"THE DONNY G STORY"

DON'T QUIT

2 | "The Donny G Story": Don't Quit

DONNY GAMBLE, JR.

ISBN 978-0692443552

Library of Congress Control Number: 2015940553

All rights reserved. No part of this book may be reproduced or transmitted in any form or by any means, electronic or mechanical, including photocopying, recording, or by any information storage and retrieval system without permission in writing from the copyright owner or publisher.

This book was printed in the United States of America.
To order additional copies contact the Publisher:
www.Hollismedia.net

TABLE OF CONTENTS

FOREWORD	5
DEDICATION	7
CHAPTER 1 Where it Began	11
CHAPTER 2 The Move	26
CHAPTER 3 A Parental View	39
CHAPTER 4 Reflections	50
CHAPTER 5 In the Midst	58
CHAPTER 6 Idealistic	65
CHAPTER 7 Donny's Perspective	70

FOREWORD

Many years ago my young son Brent came home from his first week of kindergarten, and asked if his new friend, Donny, could come over on the weekend to play. At that time, I had a private home daycare service, and we had children of all ages coming and going all the time. I was thrilled Brent had already met someone he wanted to have over to the house.

I immediately agreed and scheduled a play date with Donny's mother to bring him over one weekend. Donny was a very slender boy, with large inquisitive eyes, who had a shy infectious smile and warm spirit; I felt an immediate closeness to his quiet nature.

As time progressed, Donny and my son became as close as brothers could become and were inseparable. The boys did everything they could together; they took networking to new dimensions by creating a group of close-knit friends where they flourished and enjoyed many good times.

As the boys grew, things did change but not between them—outside of their little loving world that they created as friends, we noticed a few times that some people seemed to treat Donny with subtle differences. In our eyes, all we saw was a clean-cut, kind, smart young boy, who unfortunately endured tremendous hardship at the hands of several adults, and some students because they refused to recognize his worth as a person. Everything about it was completely wrong and dastardly in a profound way.

Young people who are hurt and provoked by their peers can generally deal with it; however, the alarming detriment is when bullying adults that have control/authority treat children unjustly that impose the most damage. It is exasperating to say the least.

In the end, these adults and others are the real losers—young people that have special talent that are overlooked and mislabeled by society often will rise up, survive, and become the winners in the world.

Babett Taylor

INTRODUCTION

DONALD and GLENDA, had the American dream, but it came at a high price, as their gifted and bright 17-year-old son's spirit had become so broken that the only peace he could find would come from thoughts of suicide. Donald's namesake, or. . . "DONNY G" had lost his will to keep on going.

This is his story as recounted by his mother and father. These events did not take place in the Jim Crow South of the 30s and 40s, nor the turbulent civil rights era of the 50s and 60s. These events occurred in the affluent Cleveland suburb of Eastlake in the past decade.

The Paradox…

After many years of hard work and determination, their persistence to get there family out of the ghetto was finally realized with the purchase of their Dream Home. In 1994, in an upscale Northern state, one would not believe that a real life "A Raisin in the Sun" could be lived out at this time, nor at this place . . . and yet it was.

Glenda is a strong-willed, supportive spouse and protective mother. Donald Sr., a strong father and husband, who takes his role as provider, and protector to heart. It is through his voice that the story of "Donny G" unfolds.

Donny G is the apple of his parents' eyes. A gifted student and all-around good kid, whose hopes of being more almost abruptly ended. His spirit severely broken by acts of racism, and brazen discrimination at the hand of educators nearly cost this family a God-given gift, their son.

We expect teens to have misunderstandings and to test boundaries among themselves to establish rank; it is a part of growing up. However, the dynamics change when adults abuse their power, and undermine the trust parents place in a system, which gives them unlimited access to influence the minds of their children.

Donny G. endures one heart-breaking episode after another until out of shear desperation concluded that his only out would be to end it all, to take his life.

The shocking reality that this joyful, charismatic, outgoing son, whose bright future was all but assured, sets the family on a new course to fight the very institution and its pernicious, insidious racial discriminatory practices that were consistently ignored.

Every conscientious parent invests in making sure their children are in a learning environment where they are intellectually challenged, and inspired to think and develop, but not at the expense of being crushed by those entrusted in academia to administer the process.

—Time after time, unconcealed racism on an institutional level (from educators) made it clear there was no place, nor interest in cultivating Donny G's talents . . . not even in sports. Despite being voted by his peers "Class" President, the teachers and administration found a loophole that stripped him of his Presidency, and made him share it with another individual. At some point, as in the poem, the dream imploded.

Unlike the climate of the 50's when such unbridled bigotry was standard in cities throughout the South, where historically as a nation there was intense struggle in race relations. However, we are not referencing 40 years ago in the rural South. No, these actual events took place a few short years ago, in the late 1990s, in an urban community in the North.

10 | "The Donny G Story": Don't Quit

♦

CHAPTER 1
WHERE IT BEGAN

♦

"The Donny G Story": Don't Quit

The story begins in 1988 in Cleveland, Ohio. It is a typical Cleveland neighborhood in economic transition, full of broken glass in the streets, abandon buildings and boarded up houses, groups of people hanging out on the corners, and seems like I could always hear sirens in the background.

We lived on an one way street that was zoned for twenty-five miles per hour; however, it was not uncommon for cars to zip through at 90 miles per hour or much faster. For that reason, most of the time, I was home; I played in the backyard which was fenced in. The fence was not put up with my older sister or me in mind; my dad and his brothers landscaped the entire backyard before we were born. They made the backyard into a basketball court that was paved with a regulation-sized hoop.

It's a 75° degrees day in June, about four o'clock in the afternoon, the sun was out and our yard is already half-full with Bros from the hood that would come over to play basketball. It would always start with three-on-three, and later four-on-four as more people came.

My uncles Anthony and J-Bone were already shooting a round and picking their teams; my dad was not home from work yet, but probably would be home soon. Since I was only four, I did not play on the big hoop—my cousins and I, along with some of the other little kids, had our own game on one of those small adjustable plastic hoops. It was fun; we could make up moves, and slam-dunk while pretending to be in the big game.

We would always dream about having the last shot to win the game with only a few seconds left on the clock. Three, two, one, he scores! Donny G made the game winning shot! It was fun to pretend, time and imagination seemed endless. They called me Donny G, named after my dad.

We lived in what they called a two-story family house. We lived upstairs, that is my dad and mom and my sister, Netta, which was short for Donnetta, and she too, was named after dad.

My parents sent us to catholic school. I guess to protect us from the public schools because we are not catholic. On this particular day, Netta has to stay late for her school recital and I do not want to go, but I know it will be impossible to get out of attending.

My grandma Lisa lives downstairs, the whole family would gather at her house for meals and other family occasions. She lived alone ever since she and Grandpa Richard were divorced years ago. Often when we played in the backyard, she would make fresh Kool-Aid and bring it out to the picnic table near the fence.

Today was no exception. Her Kool-Aid was always deliciously sweet and with everyone grabbing a cup, it was all gone in just a few seconds. All the neighborhood kids were very respectful and would tell her, "thank you Ms. Gamble." She would say "you are welcome," and then she would watch some of the basketball games with special admiration for her sons. She was so proud.

Both Anthony and J-Bone played on the same team and worked up one heck of a sweat as they were just finishing their second win. They gloated with their shirts off and flexed their muscles, and then Bone cries out, "who is next?" As if on cue, a cameo appearance by the leading man from the foot of the driveway stepped center-stage and says, "I Am!"

It was my dad, just getting home from work. Dad worked at the steel mill and you could tell. He wore these big steel-toe boots with a metal flap on top. He had this black stuff on his face and his clothes were covered in dirty grime. The black soot on Dad's face made his white teeth sparkle when he smiled; the distinction was stark because the soot was similar in concept to a black velvet canvas that a painter would use to create a masterpiece… in this case, it was his pearly whites on exhibit.

Giving dap to the bros and neighbor kids he would taunt us by saying "Y'all ready to be schooled?" He was always confident he would win.

"You don't look like any baller," Anthony said jokingly, and mocking how dad was dressed. "You just watch" dad said. "Just give me a few minutes to change."

Dad turned and saw Lil Tony, a few others and myself standing in the yard; he walked over and said, "How are you guys doing today?" "Ok," we replied. Dad said jokingly, "I will be back to school you all too." As dad turned to go upstairs, one of us said softly, "you ain't gonna school nobody." He turned around suddenly and acted as if he was going to chase us; we laughed and scattered like ants. "You ain't gonna catch nobody with those big boots on dad," I said. We all were laughing like crazy.

Life seemed limitless; we were poor and living in the hood, but for now, at this moment, I did not have a care in the world.

Dad then headed upstairs to our part of the house. As he got to the top of the stairs mom said, "Take your shoes off before you come into the house." At the top of the stairs, there was a small area with a rug where everyone placed their shoes. Of course, dad took off his boots before entering the house to keep mom from going nuts.

The way our home was constructed the kitchen was the first room that you entered from the hall, and as he turned, he could see mom washing dishing with her back to him. He eased over to her and acted as if he was going to hug her, and kiss her with that smut from the steel mill on his face, clothes and hands. "Give me a kiss beautiful" dad said. Mom turned around and she looked like a deer in headlights.

"Negro," she said insistently, "you better get away from me and go get yourself cleaned up."

It was so funny—dad was a sight. Fortunately, the bathroom was right next to the kitchen and dad proceeded in there and began freshening up; he left the door open so he and mom could still talk.

"How was your day?" He asked.
"It was busy as usual," mom said.

Mom worked as an administrator at a nearby college. It is obvious to see why dad married her; she is very attractive, light-skinned, with hazel eyes and brown hair. Simply beautiful.

Mom went on to ask, "Don I know you are not getting ready to play ball, are you?"

"I was thinking about it," dad yelled as he comes out of the bathroom just about dressed in his basketball attire.

Mom then reminded him of the family's already packed schedule for the day; "Netta is having her recital this evening and dinner is almost ready," she said. She looked up at him briefly; his smile slowly began to disappear.

"Alright" she said, "you got a half hour and don't let me come out there to get you," she smiled weaving her head, and with her hands on her hips pretending to be tough. Dad then said sarcastically, "yes dear," and then headed out back to give lessons.

As soon as dad came out the door, J-Bone said, "Come on pippin, we're up." When they began playing, Lil Tony, my other friends, and me stopped shooting on the little plastic hoop because Lil Tony said he was tired. So we sat on the back steps and watched dad and the others play.

The competition was heating up as dad just hit a 20ft shot. The guys trash talking began getting louder, so loud, that grandma Lisa came out.

"Play nice," she said in a firm voice. "Play nice," she said a second time in a louder voice. "Ok," Don and Tony said. The others agreed then went back to playing, but still grumbling.

All of a sudden, a dude I had never seen before was running up the driveway towards the backyard with a bag in his hand. Before I could say anything, he knocked over the table and Kool-Aid, which hurled the glasses and chairs all over the place.

Just as Grandma looked back, it was too late for her to move out of the way as he ran into her on the way by. He bumped into her so hard causing Grandma to fall against the steel graded fence before tumbling to the ground. He ran past all the people standing nearby, scaled the back wooden fence, which was about six foot high, intended to stop the ball from going into the neighbor's yard. Suddenly, out front, a police car pulled up.

The officer shouted, "Did you all see a guy running this way?" The person we call Tin-man said, "Yeah, he jumped the wooden fence and headed towards Yeakel Avenue," which was the next street over.

"He just robbed the corner store," the police officer said. Then he grabbed his car radio and broadcasted, "Suspect on foot, fleeing toward Yeakel Avenue, please pursue." Then he put his car in drive and sped off in pursuit of the robber.

Meanwhile, Grandma Lisa, still on the ground is attempting to gather herself. "What is wrong?" Mom screamed from the upstairs window. "Grandma looks hurt," I said. Then dad said, "Call 911." Everyone stopped playing ball and circled around Grandma, seeing if they could help. She was bleeding on the left side of her head and she seemed to be a bit incoherent. Bone said, "Someone get her a chair and a glass of water." Just then, mom came down and said to dad, "Don the ambulance will be here in a few minutes." "Thanks dear," he replied.

"Y'all can go home, we got if from here," said Anthony to the ballers. "We will see you," they said as they slowly dispersed one-by-one except Tin-man. "I am staying till I see her in that ambulance," Tin-man said. Tin-man was like family since he hung around the yard so much. He was much older than most of the fellows; probably was thirty something, but he didn't play basketball. He collected scrap in a shopping cart and I think that is how he got his name.

"That's cool," Bone said, as we sat grandma in the chair. Mom asked dad, "Don what about Netta's recital?" I am going to follow the ambulance to the hospital and meet you all after that. Mom sighed a little and then said, "Ok" while gathering her belongings.

"I'm going with dad," I said.
"Me too" said Lil Tony.
"No you're not," mom said with a sharp tone. "You are going with me, and Lil Tony has to go with his dad; he has school tomorrow you know."

Just then, the ambulance arrived and there was a feeling of relief that everything was going to be all right. The paramedics got out of the truck and came over to grandma and began treating her, and asking a bunch of questions. Finally, they put her on the stretcher and into the ambulance. Dad said to the bro's, "I'll call y'all from the hospital once I get an update." "Ok" they replied. Then dad turned towards mom and me and said, "I will see you at Net's school as soon as possible; I will be there."

Today it turned out to be beneficial that dad parked on the street instead of the driveway; the guys were still parked in the driveway and he would have spent more time waiting for everybody to move their car before he could leave. As dad was approaching the street, he began a slow jog towards his car.

Suddenly I hear, "Are you coming to the program dressed like that?" Mom shouted out to dad with a slight smirk on her face and holding a bag, which contained a change of clothes; he was still in shorts and a tee shirt.

They met half way for dad to get the clothes, exchanged a quick kiss, and he was off.

Mom and I were sitting anxiously at Netta's recital; it was still uncertain if grandma was doing okay or if dad would indeed make it in time from the hospital. Dad came in a little later. "Just in time dad" I said. "Netta will be up next."

"Cool" he said.

Mom asked, "How is Ma?"

"She is going to be ok," Dad said. "However, the hospital is keeping her overnight for observation."

Netta's entire program appeared as though it was going to last forever, which I was not happy about at all. Our neighbor, Ms. Harper, dropped off mom and me earlier while dad went to the hospital.

I think Ms. Harper is almost too old to continue driving—I'm so glad we are riding home with dad. I am just saying.

As we were riding home, and after a hundred praises to Netta from mom and dad about how good her performance was, I could finally concentrate on something else.

It was somewhat late and it didn't take Netta long to fall asleep on the way home… Mom and dad thought that I was sleeping too, but I was just sitting back with my eyes closed. Mom said to dad softly, "That situation at home earlier was scary, don't you think?" Dad said, "Yes" in a low voice, trying not to wake us.

Mom asked dad, "Perhaps we could move into our own house, in a better neighborhood, you think?"

Dad got very quiet, probably thinking (no way), but he didn't want to come across to mom like that so he didn't say anything. When dad finally got ready to speak, mom said, "Tell you what, I will make you a deal." Dad although driving, all of a sudden began making a lot more eye contact with mom.

Dad asked "What kind of deal?"

She said, "If you buy me a new house, I will have another baby for you."

To my surprise, dad's face lit up and he said with excitement, "Have another baby!" Mom smiled nodding her head—as dad drove, he continued making eye contact with mom, and then would quickly look at the road as if in total disbelief. I was surprised that dad seemed happy about that because I didn't know he wanted more kids. I later found out that he wanted seven or eight when he and mom first got married. Mom had never told dad, but somehow I knew that many kids would be out of the question.

Dad, whilst acting brain dead after mom made the proposition, finally made it home. As we were pulling up in the driveway, he asked mom, "Can we start making the baby tonight?" I said "Oooh"; they were both stunned and turned then said simultaneously, as if rehearsed, "I thought you were asleep." Then dad began to hit me with some play punches; he had a big, half-embarrassed sort of smile on his face because I heard him ask mom about starting the baby making tonight, then says, "Wake your sister up, then help your mother get the things in the house while I park the car."

As I got out of the car, I noticed stuff was still scattered all over the yard from the incident; several glasses, the picture with Kool-Aid, chairs etc.; it looked like a tornado had hit.

Mom had to carry Netta upstairs; she was still half-asleep and couldn't walk. After parking the car, Dad and I straightened up the mess even as we still played fake boxing on the side.

25 | DONNY GAMBLE, JR.

♦

Chapter 2

THE MOVE

♦

Several weeks passed and everything is returning to normal; Grandma's bruises are slowly healing, and that person who robbed the store and knocked grandma down the police arrested.

Unfortunately, Netta and I were somewhat confined. Because even though we were out of school for the summer, we still had to be up early to go to work with mom — wait at her job for over an hour, then walk to day camp. What a bummer.

The schedule was not conducive at all to being on summer vacation – it was a chore. After about five hours per day at camp it was back to mom's job, and wait around until it was time to go. What was worse, mom usually had stops to make after work that prolonged the day.

On this day when we got home, dad's car was there, which was highly unusual. Dad is never home before us. He works on the Westside and goes to night College, so we do not see him this early too often. Mom looked surprised and concerned.

When we came in dad was sitting at the kitchen table, sort of holding his head and looking at some papers. Upon Dad seeing us, he got in a hello, and then mom began bombarding him with a quick left, right, left barrage of questions. It was akin to a verbal boxing match.

"What are you doing home so early; Are you alright. You didn't get fired did you?"

"No, no, no to all of that," dad said. "I talked to a realtor earlier today. Her name is Francis. She gave me these papers to look over and she wants to begin showing us some houses this weekend."

"I'm glad that was it," she said, as she began to smile looking relieved.

"Just make sure you keep your end of the bargain" dad said, smiling as he dodged the play backhand that mom was throwing at him. Mom's smile slowly disappeared as she asked the obvious — "What about your mother?"

"I don't know," dad said, "we can't leave her here. We would have to get some place big enough for all of us."

"But, how will we afford it?" mom asked. "As you know, she wants her own space and has made that very clear. In addition, are you sure that she wants to move — did you even ask her?"

"Not yet" dad said. "I wanted to start looking first to make sure that we will have some place for sure."

Then, the hunt began. Many times just dad and mom looked, along with the Realtor of course. Other times Netta and I were able to go as well. This went on for months. At first, an anomaly always kept them from moving forward; either an issue with the neighborhood, the price or something they felt just was not right; mom or dad would get a feeling. For the most part Francis showed mom and dad properties in our county, in the city as well as the suburbs. The city was where the neighborhood was a problem and the suburbs cost was an issue.

It is about 7:30 a.m. Saturday morning, and nobody is awake but me. Being up very early was one of my favorite times because I didn't have to compete for the TV or protest which channels to watch. In addition, I am able to enjoy my big bowl of cereal and milk without interruption. The rest of the family usually starts getting up around ten a.m.

I enjoyed sitting alone to watch several of my favorite shows. However, today my mind is on other things like, will I like living in a different house, or in a different neighborhood? Alternatively, will I make new friends? Will I live too far away to visit my old friends? Etc. It is times like this when being a kid is tough. Parents make the decisions; all we can do is go along for the ride.

One by one, they get up, except Netta. Greeting each one individually I said, "Morning dad; morning mom"; although I could see that Netta was still in bed said, "Morning Netta, morning Netta" (she pretended not to hear me). I knew she was ignoring me, "morning Netta!" That little devil is just playing sleep; I will fix her.

Dad finally says, "Come on Netta get up, we have to leave in a little while, Francis will be here at noon." She rolled over slowly and sat up in the bed. "Ok daddy" she says— talking and sort of yawning and stretching all at the same time. She is such a faker— she knew she heard me calling her. Donnetta had her own room. I slept on the couch in the living room; it had a pull out bed that I never used. It was too much work for me to sleep on the pull out and have to put back all the pillows each night. Besides, when we move, I will probably have my own room.

Once Netta got up, I ran to the bathroom and pretended to wash up and as always, Netta was right on my heels. I got to the bathroom and closed the door and Netta's outside the door banging and pleading for me to let her in. Meanwhile, I stood inside laughing because I knew she would have to go when she got up and I already went earlier. Serves her right for not answering me. "Come on Donny," she yelled "let me in."

Eventually I was going to let her in, but I wanted to have fun with this as long as possible. Our house was designed that you could go thru the kitchen to get to the bathroom. Mom was cooking breakfast, and of course, taking this all in to see if we would resolve it without her.

Finally, when Netta sounded like she was ready to pee on herself, mom intervened and said, "Donny would you please let your sister in the bathroom?"

"Oh, okay mom."

Darn it, I guess I have to let the little *weed* in – although she deserved to suffer a little.

I opened the door as slowly as I could, and got sheer delight as Netta came rushing in, pushing me out and closing the door, almost all in one motion. After I came out of the bathroom, I made my way over to the kitchen table and sat down.

The air was filled with the aroma of bacon and eggs, sausage, grits, toast and coffee for dad. Mom asked, "Donny what are you going to have?" "Everything," I said with a big smile. Mom's breakfast was the best. In just a little while, we were all seated having breakfast and all the talk of course was about moving, and what area would be best for the family, etc.

It was almost noon and Francis was right on time. However, on this particular day Francis had a look of sheer determination. "Mr. and Mrs. Gamble, let us look at some properties this weekend that are in your price range but are just outside this county." As Francis spoke, she simultaneously showed mom and dad photographs of properties along with descriptions and price ranges.

Mom, dad and Francis were seated at the kitchen table while Netta and I were playing in the living room, located right next to the kitchen. We acted as if we were playing cards but, we were actually listening to find out when and if we would have to leave early; it was a Saturday morning, and since there was no day camp, the later we would have to leave the better. I would get to watch cartoons a little longer. Hooray!

When it was time for us to leave, we piled into Francis' car and the search continued. She was going to have us look in the next county so dad said, "You guys just relax we might be riding for a little while."

Dad and the realtor sat in the front, and Netta, mom, and I in the back. At first mom sat near the door on the passenger side, Netta in the middle, and I sat behind the driver's side. Without fail, the chaos started:

> "You're touching me," squealed Netta.
> "I'm not touching you" Netta (So I scooted over more to make sure).
> "Yes, you are still touching me, Donny."
> "No, I'm not touching you."
> "Yes you are."
> "No, I'm not."
> "Yes you are, and get your finger out of my face";
> "But I'm not touching you, Netta."
> "Yeah, but you got your finger in my face."

Finally, dad was undeniably tired of us razzing says, "Will you two cut it out." Mom said, "Netta move over near the door." Mom and Netta changed places, now mom was in the middle so that little charade was over with nothing for us to do but ride, and look out the window.

While mom, dad and the realtor were having a short conversation about directions, I glanced over to notice Netta was saying something in a raspy voice

(That was her way of talking when she thought she won an argument and did not want our parents to hear).

We both rather smiled while I thought to myself that I would get you next time. We were riding for a long time, the next thing I knew they were waking me up, saying "Wake up; we are here at the first house." We spent a lot to time getting in and out of the car as my parents were inspecting each house: "This one is too small, back in the car" or "this one is on a main street, back in the car" and "this one is too big" they said, and so on. That is how it went all day. Now it was starting to get dark and we were beginning to get irritable.

"I'm hungry," Netta said. "I'm tired," I said. "Hold it down" dad said. "We are going to look at one more house then we will get something to eat on the way home."

So we rode for about ten minutes and arrived at a nice house on a neat looking street, in a well-groomed neighborhood. It was hard to see the exterior of the house very well because it was almost dark, and the lighting was dim except for the occasional streetlights that were slowly coming on. There were no sidewalks; the street had sort of a trench that went from one driveway to the next. However, we did get a good look at the inside.

"Let's start off on the main floor," Francis said. We entered the house thru the side door, went up a couple of steps into the kitchen. "This is the kitchen," Francis said. I thought to myself, I could probably sell houses, everybody knows what a kitchen looks like. Then she said, "And this is the living room." At that point, it was going too slow, and intuitively Netta and I took off running thru the rest of the house. The house was a three-bedroom ranch. Mom and dad, who were still in the living room talking to the realtor, could hear us claiming our turf.

"This is my room," I said. The other room had pink walls "This is mine," Netta said. No argument there, I don't like pink walls anyway. As mom and dad looked through the rest of the house, Netta and I remained vigilantly optimistic. Perhaps this one would be our new home.

After a while dad said, "This house has much of what we are looking for except mom needed her own area. Francis smiled and said, "That's the surprise. It listed an in-law suite downstairs." Once again, the race was on between Netta and me to see who could get downstairs first. The first thing we said was, "Ooh, look, there is another whole house down here." There was a bedroom, bath, kitchen and a living room. It seemed like an eternity before mom, dad, and the realtor finally came downstairs. Mom and dad examined each room carefully, but were much quieter than I expected. Francis rather stayed out of their way to allow them to settle their feelings about the house. They looked and looked, and had these little private conversations with each other, as they often do when they both have to agree on something.

Finally, dad looked over at Francis and said, "We are very interested in this house. It has all of the amenities that we were looking for; however, we just wondered if we could afford it." Francis said, "The house is listed for eighty-seven thousand dollars, but let's offer seventy-nine thousand, nine hundred dollars."

"How much would we need down?" Mom asked. "Usually twenty percent down which comes to about sixteen thousand dollars," Francis said.

"Sixteen thousand dollars?" Dad snarled, almost yelling, and then stood there with a blank look on his face. "Where in the world am I going to come up with sixteen thousand dollars?"

"Don Gamble" mom said sharply, and giving that look, which meant she thought dad was being disrespectful to Francis.

Frankly, Donnetta and I thought it was hilarious and we were doing everything that we could to keep from busting into laughter.

"I apologize for that outburst" dad said in a low embarrassed voice. "Don't worry" Francis said, "There may be a 1st time home-owner programs available to reduce and perhaps defer part of the down payment. So if you like the house I will put in an offer and contact you in several days fair enough?"

Dad looked at mom, who was smiling and nodding her head with a show of approval, suddenly he looked at us — we were all smiles too. Dad turned back to Francis and said, "Well, I guess it's settled then."

We busted into a loud cheer. Then dad interrupted to say "Don't you guys get too happy just yet. Let's see if we will be able to get it first and then get happy." I settled down a little, but if I know mom and dad as I think I do, they will find a way to get it done.

38 | "The Donny G Story": Don't Quit

♦

CHAPTER 3
A PARENTAL PERSPECTIVE

♦

From a Father's Perspective

Donny Jr. has always been a well-mannered kid, and now, he is a fine young man. I could not be more proud. Growing up he was a kind kid, with a great disposition… good-natured.

He was reared attending church at a very young age that played a huge part of his development and as he got older, he did not venture too far away from our foundational teachings. Also for a while, he sang in the children's choir. He never resented church as a kid, and now as an adult, he is still very active in the church. He was obedient, even-tempered, and independent thinking. He has never needed to follow the crowd, or do something just because everyone else was doing it. My son was an innovative thinker and that was reassuring to us.

On the surface, he seemed shy, so much so, that until this day associates are surprised to know that we have a middle child (because he was very quiet around some folks). Donny G is definitely his own person; family members and close friends would not be able to tell too much about him. My son found his rhythm to life and certainly followed that beat (he practiced staying out the fray that didn't uplift his outlook on life).

Growing up he was fun loving, and played around just like any other child. Because my wife and I were still struggling we lived in the inner city earlier in his life, and he saw many of the things children in the ghetto often see that included limitations and lack of access to extra curriculum activities.

Although he had a basketball hoop in the backyard and all the neighbors came over to play, for a brief period he grew up where there was broken glass, abandoned houses, and unfortunately, illegal deals made at the corner and so on.

As a father, one of my darkest moments was watching my son emotionally spiral downward during high school … several events led up to him falling into a murky place. Parenting isn't an easy function by itself, and having to deal with your child being psychologically and emotionally abused by adults is an even tougher cookie to swallow. I survived the ghetto and worked hard to get my family to this point and now my son, my namesake, is entertaining thoughts of killing himself; where did I go wrong — and why is this happening?

It was reprehensible to learn of the tactics used to suppress and dissuade my son from excelling in sports. What sensible human being does this to a child?

I could not believe how much the basketball coach and other faculty members were involved in attempts to destroy my son's spirit. My dilemma was do I punch these guys out and possibly get arrested, which means my family would lose or do I put on a diplomat's hat and try to reason as a father, and as a man. Please don't misconstrue my temperament, I was mad as hell and many times it would not have mattered but I have a wife, and children who depended upon me so I could not afford merely to allow my emotions to rule the day. Nevertheless, something had to change.

As a man, and a father, my spirit would not allow me to rest without addressing the basketball coach, so I paid the chum a visit.

After having a long talk with my son that next day, I was at the school at about 6 a.m. to talk to the coach, and had to wait over an hour. I stood right at the doorway to eliminate the chance of missing the opportunity to be the first thing on his agenda. When the coach opened the school door, and came in and saw me, he looked very surprised.

Coach said nervously, "Oh, Oh, Mr. G, I will be right with you," he ran into his office, and locked the door. When the coach finally emerged and opened the door, he had three assistants with him. It was a mystery how they magically appeared with the coach since none of them walked by me (I believed they crawled through a window in the coach's office). The coach proceeded to ask "Now Mr. G what do you want to talk about?" in a smug tone.

Why he felt the need for this level of reinforcement is beyond my ability to understand, I needed to talk to him man-to-man about his handling of my son. He was just one on my list...I had one more personality to deal with, the principal. He allowed the chaos to escalate to this level by not upholding any moral standards or demonstrating leadership.

I did have my meeting with the principal despite his attempts to shrug off the concerns; I made my point very clear about my son.

Of course, the outcome could have gone either way but I constantly reassured myself that this was right, and being quiet will only fuel the flames if I waited for the administration to take courage to do the right thing.

As far as my son, Donny G, I persistently reminded him how much both his mother and I loved him, and that nothing was worth quitting over. We are winners! Therefore, we live like winners.

Without question, my wife and I were very protective of our family and made sure we did not buckle, and in the end, we were able create a better path for them to excel.

From a Mother's Perspective

I think as a mother and as the bible instructs us, "Train up a child in the way he should go and when he is old, he will not depart from it." (Proverbs 22:6)

If all parents would follow this scripture, our kids today would not easily succumb to the derisions from external forces. Instilling what God says would strengthen their foundation and give inner peace that no matter how turbulent situations are at times, they are not alone. As a mom, this is reassuring knowing that while I cannot always be present every hour of the day with my children, that there is a higher power protecting them; it is important to remind them of this.

I am not the perfect parent, but I did bring up my children in the church (which for our family is the foundation of truth). Teaching them at a young age that there is a higher being (God), then us, and he will never leave you or forsake you.

His Dad and I etched in stone never give-up or give in to negative beliefs that helped Donny excel in his undertakings. In addition, for him to know that his family is in his corner and love him unconditionally…having this reassurance is what provided tremendous strength for Donny during the darkest moments of his life.

When we bought our first home in Eastlake, a suburb of all whites, I thought my husband was crazy. I know I wanted the best for my children and they deserved to be in a nice school system just like anyone else. However, I wasn't sure at the time it was a good idea to be the first African American family to move there. As previously mentioned, it was our foundation, which is the church that helped me to keep the faith that everything would be well although some folks made waves about our presence.

Notwithstanding, we did have several unpleasant issues to address that were racially motivated; my children being the most precious gifts we have, nothing was ever going to disrupt my family's goal that we struggled to obtained that would thwart the best chance for our children to get ahead. I mean nothing!

My family dealt with everything that came our way concerning my daughter and Donny G from first thru 12th grade. By the time my youngest child was in the school system we were well known among many people, and our neighbors were more socially acceptable so the youngest didn't have to deal with a lot of racism, and bullying . . .

Getting back to the story at hand, from 1st grade through middle school, Donny G had developed a friendship with a neighbor's son, (Andy). They became real close friends. They bowled together and were in the Cub scouts together.

Actually, Andy was the youngest of three brothers who did not spend much time with him. So when Donny G appeared, Andy spent a lot of time at our house going places with us. We tried to keep Donny G active in school and the community, so he would always know that just because you have a different skin color, does not mean you cannot be a part of the same things that others enjoy.

He was a cub scout, played baseball, basketball, and when he was age 5, started on a bowling team. Again at this point, he and his sister were the only African Americans in the neighborhood and the community. Both my daughter and Donny G started school in Eastlake from kindergarten to high school. Throughout the years, they created many friendships that helped develop confidence in themselves and others.

We had a few unpleasant situations with different individuals; some felt we didn't belong in this nice neighborhood and that my children couldn't possibly do well enough to excel or weren't deserving of having a better environment. Nevertheless, we never allowed things to continue too long without confronting the problem. Over time, we ended up buying our second house, which was a lot nicer than the first one in Eastlake. It seemed that once we had one of the nicer homes in Eastlake that my children became very popular. They would always bring their friends over to the house and show them around.

We never took for granted that we were blessed to achieve what so many parents wished they could provide for their family; a stable environment, a cultural journey that afforded numerous opportunities to have exchanges with folks from different walks of life in a structured setting, and to absorb an enriched environment without thuggish interaction.

My husband and I never allowed our children to lose sight of their educational goals, and never hesitated to be the reinforcement they needed to keep the ship righted.

49 | DONNY GAMBLE, JR.

♦

Chapter 4

REFLECTIONS

♦

The old maxim still resonates "Hindsight is twenty-twenty" and "What we fail to remember we often repeat" (especially stupid stuff). I refused to be derailed by prejudice and kept telling myself I am good enough for anything. I never fully understood my parent's struggle early in life; how they pulled everything together to afford what we had. However, what I do know is for the love of family, they made magic happen for us... no matter how many things went wrong, together, they figured it out.

Getting older it is clear to see how kids are sometimes unappreciative, especially when you have great parents; they make your path smoother to travel.

However, kudos to Dad and Mom for valuing family above everything else. Knowing so many young black males who never knew their fathers, let alone, having one who participated at every level of development and challenged limitations, and gave the gift of responsibility to get up and make it happen kind of examples, inspired me to take life more seriously.

I do not pretend to be a black superman where I cannot show or express my emotions. I know in my heart that if my parents, either one, had walked away from their responsibility of parenting and selected to party their way through our developmental years, or try to be my best friend in lieu of being my parents, life would have indisputably been very different for my siblings and me.

In the hood, there is a plethora of social ills that many parents overlook and allow their children to figure out on our own. This common ghetto experience is a disadvantage to kids who have nothing, and more often than not, having absentee parents is a major cause for furtherance of their plight.

When you are frazzled and struggling for bare necessities, the uncertainty can make you throw both hands up and say, "Forget it!" But you can't.

Life is not fair… the ecosystem is brutal…

I can't gloss over the harsh reality of how down so many folks are, likewise, I will not omit to *accentuate* (highlight) the importance of having faith when nothing is there; to believe and apply your faith through hard work to get beyond where you are. That I do know. I saw it in action through my parents, and when the chips were down, and they were many times, they did not give up.

Why God blessed me to be born in this family I will never know, but I do understand God does not do random. He predestines. Being blessed to have involved parents that shaped my siblings and me is an invaluable gift. Sometimes I may not have fully understood the value of what they represented then and still do in its *totality*, however, as I journey through life and face certain challenges I am reminded of one of life's lessons they taught us; to never run from difficulty… face it, assess it, and then give your all.

Writing this book unleashed a phenomenal experience; I discovered a reservoir of dormant power just by being nostalgic that was unused. *When I intentionally took time to remember "life" in my family . . .* unknown to me at the time, I was signaling to the universe I am ready for more … I APPRECIATE what you have given thus far and can handle more. One universal principle we may not give much thought to is "we attract more of what we appreciate."

Whether I understood it not, it positioned and inspired me to pass the blessings on to the next one, and then next one, to fight for the underdog and utilize my talents for the right causes to inspire change.

In sharing my personal story I realized I could help so many that are without a compass become trailblazers in their own right, to fight back even when the fight has dwindled to a pulp.

This project created a deep reservoir of joy that helped me to slow it all down and simply appreciate life's gift. "Life" itself. We all get busy and there is always something to do, but there comes a time when you must slow it down.

If my parents had left me to my own devices everything would have been different… everything. I cannot underestimate this. It is apparent that my parents are enshrined in my heart, and I will forever salute them because of the manner in which they nurtured, and helped me to believe in myself. I count my blessings.

As my appreciation for life, my family, and God increased, so did my confidence. No matter how dark many days were, my family was always a driving force that inspired me to see beyond external distractions.

My parents constantly reminded me that there was a bright side to everything; that a miracle always existed in the midst of chaos.

However, thanks to the CREATOR, I escaped the trenches of poverty and moved so far beyond many of the social ills that thousands of young black males fall prey to, primarily absentee parents.

I can only *imagine* how much pressure they both endured that was never articulated to us children, demonstrating to us we have power to create our own energy, to own our individual destiny and never make exceptions for low energy, and limited thinking people to steal your thunder.

I embody their contributions…

The parents who feel as if they cannot take another day not having resources, being unappreciated, perhaps unemployed or under employed, listen, you have to win this battle; you cannot allow indecisiveness and doubt to trump you.

I cannot fathom what my life would be like if they had not invested themselves — instilling a strong foundational belief that GOD is an important source you want and need in your life. To embrace him, believe in him, trust him, and know without any doubt that he will never leave you without answers, proved my redeeming factor in every difficulty.

… Nothing could ever replace the example of having two engaged parents that fought for what was principle for their children, who solely depended upon them and refused to settle for anything less than stellar.

It is a cancer in our community when we allow the least of them to continue without guidance, to live without ever having a positive support system, food to eat, clean clothes, and access to a great education system. The measurements are if we select to look the other way and not involve ourselves, the dissonance will only increase and contaminate everything that is good. Somebody has to step up and own the landscape.

As you get older, you eventually are cognizant of what good fortune is — you know what it feels like to be loved. See, I am not oblivious that we were once a poor, struggling family in the hood, but GOD!

57 | DONNY GAMBLE, JR.

♦
CHAPTER 5
In the Midst of It All
♦

I remember asking myself why were so many negative things happening to me all of a sudden; why is life or at least during this period so darn difficult? As a kid I just wanted to have fun; play hoops, look at girls, hang out with my friends, and do "*normal*" things a young boy enjoy doing.

As I mentioned in an earlier chapter, it was always a great time to have my dad shoot hoops with us; he rallied the strength to make time for us despite working hard all day. This was priceless.

Cleveland, similar to all metropolitan cities has several tough areas… and we survived that. I'm grateful that both of my parents devoted themselves; they made sure we understood the importance of being alert, to assess our surroundings and if the need ever demanded, that we get out of harm's way.

Growing up in the hood was challenging by itself without any extras thrown in the mix, but there was always difficulty with several of the neighborhood troublemakers; these guys always refused to obey the law and just simply do the right thing. People like this unfortunately mark every black youth in America as being part of the systemic problem; black men are still viewed negatively in many narrow sectors in society because of another black man's behavior.

Of course, we have more black men who are corporate chairmen, political pundits, and yes, a black in charge at 1600 Pennsylvania Avenue in D.C. however, the landscape of racism and cynicism still hasn't eluded him. Mr. Obama as the most powerful man in the United States was called a "liar" publicly during his first "State of the Union" address when Representative Joe Wilson, a southern politician from South Carolina riddled the congressional chambers with "You Lie." Calling the president a liar before the entire world.

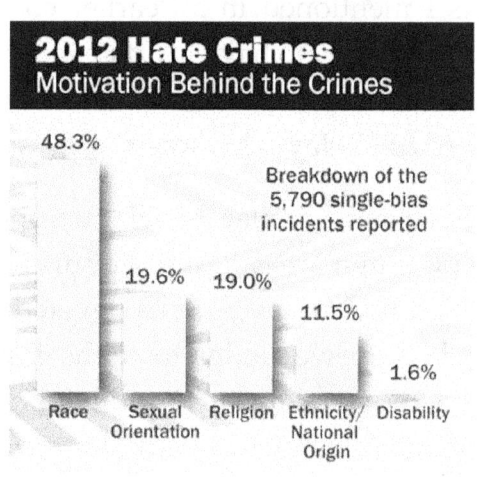

America's fluctuation with race and intolerance should be so far at the bottom of our social ills, but as the graph above reflect, skin color still matters. What are we afraid of? The God-given ability to live life abundantly full is divine, and does not warrant external approval from what was once considered the "ruling class." America's history is full of stories of systemic entrapment that was created to prevent different races from excelling.

I thank God that I did not end up bitter because of the racist bigots that persecuted me (as a kid); the narrow-minded extremists who would have loved to see me fall apart were sorely disappointed. I survived their erroneous ideology and came out better. My parents would not allow injustice to prevail … they taught me not to quit. They never did.

African Americans want the same opportunities to provide the best in life for their families, to educate their children in the best halls of academia and live in a safe neighborhood. There is no difference.

My father, a peculiar man, understood what it meant to build a platform for the next generation; he never allowed limited thinking people to thwart what he wanted to accomplish. After many years of struggling at the grind working for others, eventually started his own business. He created something he could call his own.

The Contrast

Many Caucasian fathers take ownership of shaping their sons' path – if he is a CEO, Chairman of the Board in some corporation, politician or community businessman;

he strategically exposes his son to a structured system and teaches him how to advance. They call favors to make sure their children have the gift of exposure - even when they know their kid does not measure up.

Likewise, many black fathers with a level of success take the same route to purposely teach and align their children to work twice as hard, to summon ten times more effort just to earn a footing on the ladder's rung to get in the door. In addition, when you get there, keep the door open for the next one by paying it forward.

Sadly, though, there are those parents without regard for life, and with absolutely no preparation whatsoever to be progressive to succeed. Each day is lived as though nothing matters and this too, is the example children see – they often become menaces.

Considering the amount of injustice I suffered as a kid in the 21st Century at the hands of supposedly educated adults, have to look at my contrast and example set by my father. He could have punched out a few, if not all, but got arrested, my family would have lost our superman, and I would still have been harassed.

I have no doubt my father felt like taking a different path to resolve my conflict at school, but what would we have gained as a family?

"Liberty lies in the hearts of men and women; when it dies there, no constitution, no law, no court can save it."

"Judge Learned Hand"

64 | "The Donny G Story": Don't Quit

CHAPTER 6
Idealistic

We all share an idealistic approach to life but realistically, you never know how events will affect your perspective long or short-term until you go through the experience. However, writing this book evoked numerous emotions thought to be settled and traumatic in nature.

As gratifying as life is, some days were a blur, my blood pressure elevated and subsided ... tears often welled up whilst I tried to make sense of what happened to me. As I periodically pause between thoughts and compose myself, am able to understand the positive aspect permeating before me; my family and I made it through some difficult CRAP! It was the unity of our family's spirit that pulled us through many emotional lows— in the minds of those racist thugs we were supposed to cow tow to intimidation and bullying however, what those dark personalities did not count on is I would not have to deal with their racism and threats alone. My family had my back and because they were involved, nothing was able to dissuade our will to win despite the xenophobic hooligans in academia.

Our family's focus was to get beyond the entire negative fray and not lose our identity as a loving, caring family. I believe many opponents felt we would give up the fight for equality as a black family from the hood: we all know the statistical data of parental absenteeism in the ghetto but my family was hands on.

Explicitly, my father wrestled with balancing the scales of justice; does one continue to obey the law when your child is methodically tortured, and emotionally abused by adults who have unregulated access to their person or unleash a can of kick butt? Of course, the latter would not have ended well for my family.

Having this opportunity to share my story supports my endeavor to speak to those who are unconsciously preyed upon by ill-advised teachers, adults, and under developed minds in society, because of the hue of your skin. Purpose to anchor yourself (and determine to win) and never allow disparagement from others to derail or erode your faith in one's self where you give up on life.

Realistically, the demons were knocking, gnawing at my will to live and perhaps you or someone you know may be suffering in silence, but you have to tell someone. Life is too difficult to live isolated from the protection and support of family and friends. Let them in.

As mentioned in a previous chapter, my life could have been a statistic: a young black male committed suicide. I won't pretend that the heated inferno didn't affect me... I was crushed and felt diminished as a kid who just wanted to play basketball by a coach with unresolved racism, and did many indescribable acts of intimidation, but as a *family* unit, my family helped pull me through by the grace of Almighty God.

69 | DONNY GAMBLE, JR.

♦

CHAPTER 7
The Donny G Story
My perspective of how it was living in an all-white Environment.

♦

From kindergarten through middle school things were pretty much ok. I knew I was different because I did not look like other people in the schools and neighborhood. At the beginning it was just my sister Donnetta and me, I believe we were the first African Americans to enter the Eastlake school system. My sister is older so she experienced a few racial situations before me. My parents were insistent in dealing with any violations intended to derail my sister's education; they made sure whatever surfaced was nipped in the bud so that I would not have to experience the same issues.

After we moved into the new neighborhood and were acquainted with the neighbors, although it took some time, but eventually when our neighbors figured out we were decent people, it pretty much made things easier for us through elementary and middle school. My sister and I were friends with the neighborhood kids that were in the same classes with us. I became real close friends with our neighbor's son, Andy, and then Brent, who lived on the next street. My parents signed me up on a bowling team where Andy and I were partners. Then they registered me for Cub scouts, baseball, basketball etc.

By being one of the first African Americans in the Eastlake school system, people became very aware of who the Gamble family were. Then during the time we were in elementary a few more African Americans relocated to Eastlake, moving into apartments. My parents were buying our house on Sylvia Drive—the first house we moved in. Because I was only five, when we moved to Eastlake this environment was all I knew. We used to live in what I was told was "the ghetto." I was too young to remember everything or know what the difference was until my parents explained why they wanted us to have a better environment.

In high school is where things started seeming very clear to me that I was not like the rest of them, and "politics" played a big part of it. After going through elementary and middle school in Eastlake, one would think that everyone knows you by now, and that you are in reality no different from anyone else other than the hue of your skin.

Although, going into high school at Eastlake was a very exciting time: a new school, graduating from middle school, etc… I had friends since the middle school (Wickliffe Middle School) which was in Eastlake as well. Being one of the few African Americans in the school, I always stood out, but managed to cultivate many great relationships because I treated people with respect and looked for the same in return. I wasn't raised in a prejudice household.

I thought since I was very popular in the community and neighborhood that high school would be smooth sailing. However, when it came to playing football and basketball, the powers-to-be let me know I was not going to be a star no matter how well I played. I played football just one year, I believe that was the 10th grade, the coach seemed to like me but he benched me most of the whole year. When I did play maybe once or twice, I helped score points. I didn't let that bother me too much but I still didn't sign up again. Having a dual sports interest, my focus directed me to try something else, and not allow those *intransigents* to ruin my dream.

I really enjoyed playing basketball so that is what I focused on. I had been playing basketball and baseball from elementary through high school. Again, most of the time I was benched in basketball, and didn't have the opportunity to help my team because the coach would not allow me.

This is when I say politics played a part in denying me access because it was obvious on the court, and in the stands (some of my teammates' parents), who influenced decisions as to whose kids played all the time, many of whom the coach shared a tight association. Even though I was frustrated and wanted to give up, my dad always coached me into never giving up. My dad was the personification of what an excellent coach represented; he believed that you never run from anything that is hard, that you face difficulty, and learn how to win against the odds.

This led me to want to run for class president. All of the students at that time suggested that I run for class president when I was in the 11th grade. So I ran and I won. Then in 12th grade, I decided to try again, and once more overwhelmingly, the students backed me.

The vote was unanimous; I was voted class president. Well, my winning the election didn't go over well with the girl who came in second place. I guess she decided that I should not have won class president her senior year, after all, how would that look on her record that an African American beat her.

So she decided along with the staff at Eastlake North High School to find a way to change that. Long story short, they decided to make both of us class presidents even though I truly won with probably 99% of the vote. This became very devastating to me to the point that all I wanted to do was graduate, and never have to be put in a situation as such. When I think back on this, and the situations that are going on in the school systems with bullying today, I realize that bullying is not just students bullying students; the unthinkable is adults are bullying students, and many administrators aren't doing anything to prevent this from happening.

In my situation, teachers put me through hell and tried to make me feel like I was not entitled to be a class president, and verbally terrorized me. They were more concerned with saving face for a young Caucasian female than being fair; I won the election, but they made me share the office.

In their minds, how would it look in the school records that the first African American in a predominately all white school system was class president. I would not be surprised if the record was changed to reflect that I was runner up. However, it does not matter too much to me now because I know the truth, and moved on. When I first entered college, again I wanted to quit because the desire to play professional basketball was no longer in my system because of the situation in high school.

The other problem I had when I first went to college was not being able to relate to people of my culture. I actually cried many times, and called my mom and wanted to run away from the pressure. It never occurred to me that I was only accustomed to being around white people and that I could not interact with my own people.

After all the mayhem, the end of my story, "Glory to God" is I finished college with a B.A. in business and a Master's degree in Marketing. I am now a successful Entrepreneur living in San Diego, and have been traveling abroad and plan to be a millionaire within the next couple of years.

I wanted this book published to let the young generation know that despite the trials and tribulations of life that everyone will endure, just don't quit your dreams, don't quit on the God gifted talents that you have been given. Go through the obstacles that will come, but don't let the obstacles stop you. Don't Quit

Family is EVERYTHING!

FOR INTERVIEWS CONTACT – PUBLISHER

The Hollis Media Group 844-483-4400

Hollismediagroup@outlook.com

ORDER ADDITIONAL COPIES –
WWW.HOLLISMEDIA.NET

"The Donny G Story": Don't Quit

www.ingramcontent.com/pod-product-compliance
Lightning Source LLC
Chambersburg PA
CBHW071742040426
42446CB00012B/2446